GO WITH YOUR GUT
How To Make Decisions You Can Trust

Mary Goulet

-SECOND EDITION-

Mary Goulet Media
Encinitas, CA

ISBN: 978-0-9832209-0-9 (paperback)
ISBN: 978-0-9832209-1-6 (ebook)

Editing and book layout by Kelly Poelker
Proofreading by Marilyn Stafford

LCCN: 2010918891

First Edition: September 2004
Printed in the United States of America

For information contact:
http://www.GoWithYourGut.net

This book is dedicated

to Jim Donovan.

.

Table of Contents

JUST SO YOU KNOW… I

MY PHILOSOPHY II

CHAPTER 1 1
WHAT TO EXPECT 1

CHAPTER 2 3
SETTING THE STAGE 3

CHAPTER 3 9
DON'T FOLLOW YOUR HEART 9

CHAPTER 4 13
DON'T BELIEVE EVERYTHING YOU THINK 13

CHAPTER 5 21
GUT KNOWINGNESS 21

CHAPTER 6 31
CONFUSION IS A GOOD THING 31

CHAPTER 7 51
THE LANGUAGE OF YOUR HEAD, HEART AND GUT
RECAPPED 51

A FEW REMINDERS...63

YOUR TRACK RECORD.......................................66

MY WISH FOR YOU **67**

YOUR GUT MOMENTS...**68**

TOOLS FOR ACCESSING YOUR GUT **69**

BONUS CHAPTER **73**
THE SOUL OF YOUR GUT 73

QUICK REFERENCE **83**

ACKNOWLEDGMENTS **87**

ABOUT MARY GOULET **89**
OTHER BOOKS BY MARY GOULET 90

Just So You Know...

Once you learn how to go with your Gut, you can't unlearn it. Even if you choose to act despite its guidance, you can't deny its voice. Going with your Gut is one of those things that falls into the "not if, but when" category of life.

Once learned, you won't have the choice "if" you'll go with your Gut, but "when" you'll go with your Gut. Believe me; get to "when" as soon as possible. It makes life much easier.

One more thing, once you learn and practice how to hear and trust your Gut, don't be disappointed when those around you don't understand or aren't pleased with your new sense of confidence and self-assuredness. After awhile, they'll get used to you not giving an explanation for why you will or will not do something, beyond saying, something tells me, or it just doesn't feel right. Give it time. Soon, they will grow to respect your instincts and trust your judgment.

My Philosophy

I believe going with your Gut is a very efficient way to live an authentic, purpose-filled, satisfying life and it's the key to inner peace and soul fulfillment. This book will tell you how to listen to your Gut.

I contend the voice of our Gut is our highest self or Soul, if you will. I also add that it can be the voice of God or whomever we may want to call it. It is the voice we pray to under stress and when we're afraid and need an answer. Answers are ever present and in the moment, and this book will help you to identify the voice that is constantly giving you guidance.

I am a practicing Catholic and a mystic. I have great respect for one's sense of spirituality and where it exists in nature. I enjoy the study of the great teachers and masters. I'm fueled by a dynamic, mystical yet practical, soulful life study quest. I've learned to follow my life rather than try to think it up.

The Go With Your Gut process is simple, and easy to grasp quickly. The hard part is acting on it. The process works and is infallible – I know that's a bold claim, but, after well over a decade of working with it, I can attest to the fact it is infallible. Sometimes that can be annoying because really, no one likes a smarty-pants and your Gut really is smart. Our Gut probably invented the phrase, "I told you so."

To add breadth and depth to the process, I've added a Bonus Chapter at the end of the book. In it, I'll address free will vs. your Soul's will, destiny vs. fate, and the ability to live from and act on your Soul rather than your personality, so you can effortlessly express your Soul.

Chapter 1

What to Expect

Go With Your Gut is a tool kit, a reference guide, and a powerful process dedicated to cultivating and strengthening a foolproof and ultimately life changing, decision-making philosophy. I'll show how your Gut, also called instinct, intuition, and Gut knowingness, is based on your own uniqueness and individuality. It's a comforting inner compass providing easy, fast and accurate answers to the questions, challenges and decisions you are facing.

Go With Your Gut demonstrates how having respect for your Gut voice allows you to let go of your resistance to change, conquer fear and doubt, and find the power to move from procrastination, confusion, and stagnation into a world of clarity, vision, action, and confidence while achieving your ultimate self expression.

> "Nobody can give you wiser advice than yourself." – Cicero

The goal of this book is to help you trust yourself more than you trust anyone else. To trust your knowingness of what works and what doesn't work for you in all areas of your life.

The first page of Ralph Waldo Emerson's essay on Self-Reliance states:

> "… else tomorrow a stranger will say with masterly good sense precisely what we have thought and felt all the time, and we shall be forced to take with shame our own opinion from another."

I'm not suggesting you don't listen to advice from friends, family, or a therapist. I am saying you know the right answer. I'm going to teach you a simple process, and once you learn it, all you have to do is remember to use it.

Chapter 2

Setting the Stage

Trust Yourself

As we've heard so many people say, trust yourself. I believe people do want to trust their judgment and feel confident in their decisions, but most admit they don't know how to on a consistent basis.

There are many books on trusting your intuition and Gut instinct, and I've read as many as I could find. I was searching for the how-to and not the softer side that leans on intuition. Yes, we do get hunches, but there is a more practical way to know the right choice in the moment. I've learned that process and am happy to report that it's simple and as I mentioned, infallible. Now, just because it's simple doesn't mean it's easy to remember to do, but it is quick to learn and easy to apply.

We're faced with decisions every day; how to know if we should take a new job, stay or leave a relationship, etc. Throughout the many books I read on intuition, they all gave me comfort in knowing we do have an inner compass that guides us throughout our day. What they didn't teach me was a concrete way to know for certain if I was hearing my Gut, and how to trust it on a consistent basis.

Overcome Fear and Self-Doubt

I started coaching individuals in 1997 on how to achieve their highest potential. It became very clear to me that we all have a fundamental fear of the unknown and that fear fuels self-doubt. Once self-doubt starts, we can't possibly trust our own judgment.

Also, another thing happens when self-doubt clicks in; we have a hard time admitting what we truly want in our life because we doubt our ability to make it happen.

Usually, a client would come to see me because an area of their life was troubling them, and they felt confused and conflicted about how to change it. During the session, I would illustrate how they could know for certain what the best choice or decision would be. That process became Go With Your Gut.

Over the course of my first year of coaching, I found it interesting that people have a hard time admitting how they want their life to be. And I realized there are a couple of reasons for that.

First, we don't like change. Secondly, we fear the unknown of our lives even if it's for a short period of time.

Change is the only constant in the Universe, and thinking we know what's going to happen moment-by-moment is just not possible. So, the solution is:

- ☺ Embrace change
- ☺ Let go of control
- ☺ Follow your Gut

Learn to Act Confidently— Moment-by-Moment

In each chapter, I've outlined what you can do to cement your Gut knowingness until it becomes second nature, allowing you to know and hear your Gut. This is possible to do. To act confidently, moment-by-moment, on your inner knowledge is empowering and exciting.

When I first began to coach others, I really wasn't following my own Gut consistently because I was learning along with my clients. However, I quickly began to pay attention because each time I went with my Gut, things in my life just worked out better and more smoothly.

In fact, for an entire year, I made a commitment to walk my talk and follow my Gut in every decision. And I mean each and every decision from the benign to the critical. That experiment has changed how I live.

Your Life Will Change As You Trust Your Gut

My relationships changed. I ended many friendships and created new friendships with people who I felt more aligned with. My work has taken on a deeper meaning. I feel more passionate and committed to my purpose, and of being of service to others using my talents, gifts, and desires, all because I've learned to follow my Gut. I'm also teaching my two daughters how to trust their instincts and knowingness.

I'm also more aware of the sabotaging and fearful thoughts that used to stop me from accomplishing what I wanted in my life. My Gut guides me on my journey through life, and your Gut is trying to guide you, too.

This is a book about courage and trust. Specifically, I will show you how to have the courage and trust to listen to your Gut, follow your instincts, and learn to trust yourself more than you trust anyone else.

By doing so, you'll learn to make decisions quickly and confidently. With the help of this newfound clarity and confidence, you can embark on a miraculous journey of self-discovery, empowerment and self-reliance, which will lead to a very satisfying and exciting life.

Going with your Gut means trusting and acting on what you already know to be the right thing to do—you know it because it comes from the deepest part of your soul—and by tuning into this innate knowingness, you unlock the tremendous forces of your talents, gifts, dreams, ambitions, purpose and destiny.

Make Your Life Easier: Go With Your Gut

Following this program will make life so much easier. You won't have to "think up" your life anymore. Just follow the clues given you during the day by your Gut. This process will be your daily companion for training yourself to notice the clues moment-by-moment.

With 60,000 thoughts a day, it's virtually impossible to follow and control what we are thinking. You can hear your thoughts; even acknowledge them, though you don't have to act on them. Instead, set them aside and notice the sensations in your body. Your body speaks to you, but you are so used to listening to your head and heart chatter that you ignore your body talk.

Moment-by-moment, each day we are making decisions and choices. It is very easy to decide if we want a sandwich or soup for lunch, or any other benign choice; but when we're under stress and the potential outcome has higher stakes, we struggle. Getting back to the sandwich and soup analogy; when you start flexing your Gut muscle you become more deliberate and even stop and check in with your Gut about something as simple as that. The result is that you are where you ought to be, doing what you ought to be doing at all times.

Chapter 3

Don't Follow Your Heart

One of the three places we make decisions from is our Heart. We're familiar with this area because this is where we "emote." Our Heart is emotional and wants to be soothed in the moment, and it will follow the stronger of the other two—our Head/Ego or our Gut. The Heart wants what it wants, to feel good now.

I'm going to tell you something controversial: Don't follow your Heart. I know this is counter to everything you've heard from your family, friends, pop-psychologists, and the movies. The truth is, your Heart is a follower, not a good leader. It cannot make the right decision on a consistent basis. Why not? Because our emotions change all the time. Surely, you can think of a time when you were mad as hell one minute and happy the next. It isn't in our best interest to bank on the Heart for good judgment. It's in charge of emotions. The Heart changes, reacts, and responds.

The Heart Offers Passions, Not Decisions

Many times when you think you're confused or you're trying to justify doing something "iffy" in the name of love, you've probably tried to convince yourself you were making a good choice by saying, "I'm following my heart." Now, there's nothing wrong with following your Heart if it's the right decision, but as I mentioned before, typically it is difficult for the Heart to choose correctly. The Heart's job is to fuel you with passion, not to make decisions or take risks.

Your Heart is the seat of feeling. A classic example of your Heart's role in a decision is when we're in a relationship. Have you ever been involved with someone you just knew wasn't right for you, but thought, maybe he will change? You probably did that because you had strong feelings about the person, despite what your Gut was cluing you in on. Remember, our Heart is not logical like our Head, so sometimes it will lead you to places that your Head would fear to go. But your Heart does have its merit and is an important part of the team: Your Head, your Heart, and your Gut.

Your Gut takes a broader view and knows it will be all right even if it's uncomfortable. It takes discipline to do the right thing. Particularly when it involves a relationship, and sometimes the right thing hurts.

We've been taught to follow our Heart. Our Heart is emotional and making decisions from an emotional place isn't always smart. It's a romantic gesture and one that only works if our Gut sanctions it first.

Chapter 4

Don't Believe Everything
You Think

From here on out, I will refer to our thinking, reasoning, and mental capacity as our Head, and this also means it is ruled by our Ego. Sometimes, I won't list Ego because it may read as cumbersome in the sentence, although the Ego is implied as synonymous or a twin of our Head and it rents real estate in our mind.

What is your Head's motivation and how does it communicate? Your Head is schooled; it learns how to think and use logic. It's where you go when you want to "figure things out." Its foundation is rooted in problem solving and doubt. It's where confusion resides and chaos begins. In your Head, you question the details and over-analyze the circumstances as you think hard about what to do. When relying on your Head, you run the risk of compromising the very things that are most dear to you, thus selling your Soul. That's made possible because you're attached to an outcome that you fear.

There are many types of fear that influence your Head. It can be the fear of social loss, physical discomfort, danger, or judgment from others. When you're in your Head you're justifying and analyzing the facts. Your Head's agenda is fear-based. "How can I avoid problems?" You might find yourself going over all the "shoulds" and "shouldn'ts" instead of going with what you really want.

Your Head Is Logical and Fear-Based

Your Head is logical and wants to keep you out of trouble. Its goal is to keep you safe as it tries to stay a step ahead in life by avoiding potential pitfalls and consequences. It's analytical in its approach to most everything it encounters. It does have its positive traits such as fact finding, learning from past experience, and attaining knowledge. However, your Head is not good at trusting that which it can't see or explain. It wants to be certain in advance of each step to ensure the safety of your being on all levels.

In defense of your Head, sometimes its logic is in line with your Gut, making it easier to justify following your Gut's guidance. But your Head won't give your Gut credit for a good decision. Your Head will incorrectly believe it chose wisely on its own. Sometimes, sticking to the facts does create success, but this doesn't mean it's the best option. At times, things appear to be logical but they still aren't true. Other times, the most logical solution is the right one. And, things are not always as they seem, so if your

Head is in control, your Gut doesn't have a chance to lead you in the right direction.

Your Head considers time its friend. If it can stall while it searches for an answer, it will. Procrastination and confusion are tactics your Head will use to avoid acting on your Gut.

Here is an example of how your Gut is clearly giving the answer and your Head is arguing with it.

Your Head Stalls For Time: Carol's Story

Carol heads up a dynamic and growing company. She takes pride in being the boss and the creative flare she expresses in her work. She loves the independence of being her own boss and has faith in her ability to lead.

The demands of sales, management, and making payroll twice a month often wear her down. She believes it's just a matter of time, though, and it will get easier. She's put a lot of time into getting her business off the ground and it has made progress.

A national company contacts Carol with an offer to run a large regional section of their business. The potential of security and a steady paycheck seems alluring, but deep down she doesn't want to lose control of her own company.

The pros and cons are clear, although Carol struggles about what to do. The company sent her a nondisclosure agreement and nine days later, it's still sitting on her desk, unsigned. Carol is stuck.

This is a classic case of knowing the answer and just not liking the options. Her first instincts told her to tough it out and continue building her business. Though flattered by the offer from the large company, she knew it wasn't the right step to take. The allure of prestige and security kept Carol on the fence. But when she went to pick up the pen and sign up, it just didn't seem right. Carol could have saved herself hours of anguish if she recognized her Gut instinct and gracefully declined the offer. Instead, she argued with herself and doubted what she knew was the best option. The experience left her feeling disempowered, unsure and insecure.

Sometimes, Your Head and Your Heart Team Up: Not Good

Your Head can also trigger emotions from your Heart. When your Head and your Heart team up, your Gut is bypassed and a drama is most likely to ensue. Your Head's reaction to fear is different than your Heart's reaction to fear. Your Head is reactionary and projects into the future the possible maladies that could take place. Your Heart will feel and have its vision clouded by emotions such as empathy, sympathy, compassion or pain.

So what do you do with your Head? You think, right? Well, that's where you get yourself into trouble when it comes to making decisions. You've been trained to think and analyze your way through life, to be logical. Thinking is the learned response that many people confuse with intelligence. Everyone is capable of thinking, but people have varying degrees of intelligence. Intelligence is rather hard to define and has more to do with the capacity for complex and abstract thought and mental acuity. Thinking is merely the act of cogitating. When you have made a mistake in the past, you've been asked, "What were you thinking? Didn't you use your head?" The truth of the matter usually is, ironically enough, you did use your Head and that's where you went wrong. You analyzed yourself away from your Gut's solution.

Your Head is not the place to go to figure out what to do, when to do it, or why to do it. Your Head is the mind's domain. It's the place you've been trained to go to make decisions based on sorting through problems, via analysis, justification, and debate. Within the realm of mind, you can talk yourself into or out of anything. You can attach varying degrees of emotion to any range of perceived outcomes, potentially spinning yourself far off the mark. You are designed to fear not having enough, to fear making the wrong decision and to fear what others would think of you. Your Head is a conformist. Your Head wants you to fit in, do what others expect of you and keep things copacetic.

Your Head often stands in opposition to your Gut. Your Head is the constantly thinking, overly analytical aspect of the Ego, which continually challenges the knowingness of your Gut. It thinks it knows best and that its duty is to preserve and defend you in the face of seemingly continual danger.

Your Head operates on fear and doubt. It deals in crisis management and manipulation. It anticipates and strives to avoid pain as much as possible. Your Head wants things to make sense. But sometimes the truth doesn't make logical sense. A common manifestation of this fear is continual questioning. Your Head often speaks in questions or sentences that express doubt. When you catch yourself starting thoughts with "how," "what if," "why," or "but," you're in your Head.

What's Your Decision-making Default

When you figure what your decision-making default is you can make better decisions, quicker and without second-guessing yourself. We all typically make decisions primarily from our Head or our Heart. If you know your default then you can make decisions faster because you'll recognize if you're analyzing something or caving into your emotions. It helps to be aware of your decision-making default.

Our Head is fear-based and makes decisions by first asking a lot of questions with sentences that start with:

- What if…?
- But, how…?
- When…?
- Why…?

Another clue that you're making decisions with your Head is that there is a 'because' in the sentence. A *because* is always positioned right after the Gut command or statement of five words or less. The reason it is there is because the Head wants to take the Truth of your Gut and turn it into what your Head wants it to be. Our Head wants to control all of the circumstances and outcomes. Our Heart on the other hand just wants to feel good. Of course, it's emotional and an example of the range of emotions include:

- Sadness
- Anger
- Fear
- Joy
- Insecurity
- Happiness
- Loneliness

To figure out if you are a Head or a Heart decision-maker pick a decision you've recently had to make and ask yourself, the following questions:

- ☺ Did you feel fearful and analyzed your options?
- ☺ Did you try to change circumstances or manipulate events and others?
- ☺ Did you worry what others would think of you?
- ☺ Did you keep asking the same questions over and over again?
- ☺ Did you try to protect yourself from feeling bad or someone else from feeling badly?
- ☺ Did you want to just walk away from the decision as it made you too uncomfortable?
- ☺ Did you become very anxious or cry?
- ☺ Did you procrastinate hoping the decision would go away?

With the exception of the third question, the first four are Head questions and the last four are Heart questions. The third one, *did you worry what others would think of you* is both a Head and Heart question.

Trust me, you make decisions predominately from your Head or your Heart. Once, you identify which one you save a lot of time.

Chapter 5

Gut Knowingness

Since your Gut knows everything it's important to learn how to trust your Gut.

I'm sure you've heard of it and may have even said you went with your Gut at times in the past. In fact, when someone makes the comment "Something tells me..." or "I have this feeling..." we understand immediately. We don't ask "What do you mean 'something tells you'?" We know what they mean. We've experienced it ourselves. Instead, we nod in agreement or simply say, "okay."

My reason for writing this book is to show you how to hear your Gut voice on a continual basis. It's always there, so why don't you use it more often? Here's the problem: you're most likely to discount your intuitive, Gut-level instincts. Right now you might even be thinking, "I don't know if I'm really hearing my Gut." When the stakes are low, you're willing to go on a hunch and say, "something just told me to do it," but when a critical decision or risk is imminent you become fearful, confused and lose clarity.

You have a built-in knowingness; you just need to learn how to listen to it and act on it. This knowingness is where the truth of who you are and what you're capable of resides. It's where you can go to find direction and answers in your life.

What is a Gut choice? A Gut choice is the most specific choice you can make for yourself at any given moment that will get you on your highest Soul path for your life. Each of us has a mission in our lifetime; the reason we were born if you will. Our highest desire to express emotionally, physically, mentally and spiritually. To sum it up:

> *Each one of us has a mission;*
> *Our mission has a purpose;*
> *Our purpose is fueled by passion;*
> *And, executed through service.*

Your talents, gifts, dreams, interests and desires are housed there. Your Gut will shed light on and support your uniqueness and individuality. Your Gut can answer the tough questions like:

- What is my purpose?
- Is this all there is?
- Should I take a chance on a new job, a relationship, or financial opportunity?

This sounds like a bold claim, but it works.

We have to make decisions that can make or break our comfort zone. What coping skills or methods do you currently rely on to ensure you'll have no regrets? There's only one rock solid approach that can encompass your faith and autonomy while insuring the best outcome for all concerned: Your Gut knows.

Gut Knowingness Is Not Psychic

Knowing your Gut is "Gut Knowingness." Gut Knowingness, the way I use it, is a synonym for intuition. I like to refer to it as Gut Instinct or Gut Knowingness because it seems more tangible and practical than the word intuition implies. Some texts on the subject of Gut Instinct or intuition go into a deep explanation of how to hear and develop meditative or psychic awareness. I want to keep things less complicated than all that.

If you're interested in developing your intuition, it certainly can't hurt, but you don't have to be highly intuitive or psychic to go with your Gut. You don't need to take a New Age kind of approach to hear your Gut. You don't need to belong to a certain religion, either. It's not necessary to find a quiet room, meditate, chant, stand on your head, fire walk, or become vegetarian to know what your Gut is saying. Some of these things might be fun, healthy or interesting; they're just not necessary when you're listening for your Gut. Connecting to Gut Knowingness or Gut Instinct is pretty basic, which is the beauty of it.

Your Gut is the place where you just know. So where does this knowledge come from? Some of it might be from past experience, some of it could come from subtle perceptions, but for the most part, let's just say your Gut Knowingness is innate. It's the silent sage inside you. There isn't anything magical or mystical about accessing your Gut for guidance; it just takes recognizing the language and sensation of it and consistently acting on it.

Gut Knowingness is clear and courage-based. Your Head and your Heart are not categorically wrong in what they guide us to do; it's just that your Gut is categorically right.

Gut Knowingness Is Not Mysterious or Esoteric

So, Gut Knowingness is linked to intuition, but it's not mysterious or esoteric. Everyone continually experiences this knowingness. The obstacles to acting on these clear messages arise when fear comes into play and we doubt this innate wisdom. Your Head latches onto fear, attempting to anticipate and manipulate all possible consequences, weighing them on a scale of personal success vs. failure. Only your Gut gives one clear, neutral answer.

It is easy to recognize the voice of your Gut. You might even feel a physical sensation deep in your viscera. The message of your Gut comes into your awareness quickly and in a complete, concise manner. You'll experience it as a moment of clarity, the eye of the hurricane, and the calm after the storm. It's that instinctual voice that everybody has heard at one time or another. You've heard it, too, but you might be afraid that you don't know how to harness it. Quiet yourself and just listen. The still, calm, steady voice of your Gut is waiting for you.

Your Gut is the deep center of your Soul that you can trust with certainty to give clarity in any situation. It will tell you what is right. It never needs explanation or justification. It has neither expectation of nor attachment to a perceived outcome. Your Gut has the same neutral response whether you're faced with a crisis or a pleasurable experience.

Its nature is calm. Your Gut speaks in a simple statement. Its goal is to guide and feed your sole/soul purpose. Your Gut nurtures and wills the Self into creation, making manifest the truth of which we are, not who we think we should be. There's no artifice, no analysis and no emotionally backed demands. Your Gut simply is.

The Language of Your Head, Your Heart and Your Gut

The best way to know if you're listening to your Head, your Heart or your Gut is to listen to the language of each one. So, when you say that you're confused or just want to be sure you make the right decision, hear what you're thinking and saying so you can decipher one voice from another. Here's an effective exercise to do that:

Write down what you hear when you're struggling with a decision. Many of us are used to listing the pros and cons of a dilemma we're facing only to end up full circle, and still don't know what to do. So here's a way around that.

Grab a tape recorder and recite your dilemma. (You can also call a friend, especially one who has read my book or has seen my presentation. They'll hear right away what you're doing.) Once you've exhausted your story, listen back and note the following:

- Were you speaking in sentences and asking questions beginning with But, What if? or How?
- Were you fearful?
- Were you trying to rationalize, justify or explain yourself?

If you answered 'yes' to any of the above you were in your Head.

- Were you emotional?
- Did you hear concern about what others would think of you?
- Were you feeling bad for someone?

If you answered yes to any of the above, then you were in your Heart. Now, both your Head and your Heart can work together which can be a bad combination as they rule out your Gut's guidance.

Lastly,

> ⊚ Did you hear any command or statement of only five words or less, with no reason why to do something, just the command to do it?

If you answered yes, then you were listening to your Gut! See how easy it is?

Truth:
Your Gut always gives you an answer first, before your Head or Heart chimes in. If it didn't speak first, your Head and Heart wouldn't have anything to debate.

Definition of Your Head, Heart and Gut – Memorize These

Your Head/Ego:
Is fear-based and likes to control a situation. It speaks in sentences and asks questions such as Why? But, how? What if? It has an agenda and is emotionally attached to an outcome. It makes excuses, explains, justifies and rationalizes so it can get its way.

Your Heart:
Is emotion-based. It's a follower and therefore not a reliable decision-maker. Its main concern is about how you and others will feel. It's sentimental and nostalgic. It's in the middle and will support the more dominant of the two, your Head or your Gut.

Your Gut:

Is courage-based. It's a visceral, instinctive knowing and it is faith at its most potent. It speaks in commands or statements of five words or less. It speaks first before your Head or Heart, always. It won't necessarily give you a reason to: Do, Don't or Delay.

The Definition of Do, Don't and Delay:

Knowing what to do always begins with patience and hesitation, the good kind of hesitation. The kind of hesitation that makes us stop before we decide to do something we want to do versus knowing what we should do. We're all used to being stimulated and on the go so we when we have a decision to make we hurry through our choices. We have to become very aware if we are choosing to do something because it feels right or if we are doing it to keep busy. When you get an impulse to do something, ask yourself, "Should I...do, don't or delay?

Do: A clear command to act. Not every "Do" will be comfortable. Sometimes they test our comfort zone and demand us to be courageous, patient and to show faith.

Don't: Again, a clear command and sense of resistance to not do what we really might want to do. We will experience instant regret when we go against a *Don't*. For example, have you ever had a *Don't* when you wanted to phone someone and did it anyway only to get a pit in your stomach and say, "I shouldn't have called." Ugh. Also, you can't undo a *Don't*.

Delay: When there isn't a *Do* or a *Don't* and you're told to wait until you get a firm Do or a Don't. Be patient with this. Rushing to a Do or a Don't has its consequences.

Chapter 6

Confusion is a Good Thing

When someone has to face a decision they don't like, they'll often say, "I'm confused. I don't know what to do." Actually, here's what's really going on:

Truth:
Confusion can only exist when your Gut is telling you what to do and you don't want to do it. That's really what it boils down to, you just don't like your options; anxiety builds from there.

Let's use a relationship issue to illustrate my point because every one knows what a red flag feels like, and your Gut guidance is the same thing. You've been dating someone for a while and find out he or she has been unfaithful. Your Gut screams, time to go and your heart cries, but I love him or her. Your Head may say, this is the only issue we have; otherwise, our relationship is great. Then you become conflicted, confused.

You really don't want to end the relationship, but you know you can't trust this person. If you would listen to and act on your Gut, you wouldn't be confused. Confusion only sets in when you began listening to your Head and your Heart as they try to convince you to ignore your Gut.

Remember: Your Gut always speaks first, period. Then your Head and Heart chime in.

When I speak to groups or coach individuals, I always get someone challenging me on this statement: Your Gut always gives an answer first. They'll ask me how I can be sure, and I'll tell them because your Gut is constantly guiding us throughout the day from the time we wake up in the morning to when we go to bed. Our Head only gets involved in the job of influence or guidance when it fears what our Gut is telling us to do or not do in the moment.

We're guided on what to do constantly throughout the day, and when a situation occurs, an answer is given immediately. Sometimes, the answer is to not do anything yet, or it gives a specific action to take or a combination of the two. Nevertheless, it gives direction in an instant.

You Always Know What To Do

The next time you're confused remember you *do* know what to do. Say this to yourself: *Confusion exists when I know the answer, but I just don't like it.* Avoid the habit of stalling in hopes that the answer will change. Maybe it will, but the circumstances will be different. Another important point: don't judge the answer.

The powerful, universal barrier we hide behind when we know what to do, but don't like our options is called *confusion*. Or at least that's what we like to call it.

True confusion arises when things are unclear, out of order, or not discernable. The story below will help you put your own definition of confusion into perspective.

Confusion About The Restroom: An Example

You're visiting a foreign country and need to use the restroom. You're standing on the corner becoming increasingly anxious as the seconds go by, looking for a friendly face to ask for directions. You make eye contact with a woman and pantomime the need to find a restroom. She clearly understands and begins rattling off instructions in broken English, pointing and gesturing in several directions. You nod, but you can't understand anything she's saying. Perhaps she was pointing to a building down the street, or perhaps not. Things are still completely unclear to you. Now, that's confusion.

Finally, someone who speaks English arrives and comes to your rescue and proceeds to tell you your restroom options. There is one restroom that is fairly close by; it's usable but it's filthy. He describes how filthy and you ask him anxiously what the other option is. There is one that is much cleaner, but it's several city blocks away. Your immediate needs are pressing and you need to make up your mind. Which one should you choose? You're annoyed because you don't like your options. Some people might call this confusion, but you actually know your options, you're just not very happy about it.

You've started to dance about and obviously won't be able to stay in that state of "confusion" for long. The odds of coming up with better options are pretty slim. You're getting increasingly uncomfortable. The choice is made from necessity, and off you run to the filthy, but nearby restroom. Whew!

So what's the moral of the story? When you don't know the facts or can't understand the directions, you really are confused. Once you actually know your options, you can make the right decision. Just because you are struggling to make up your mind doesn't mean you're confused. What it does mean is something very different. You know what you are looking at; you just wish it were something different. And confusion is the perfect excuse for your Head to start the convoluted process of analysis it so loves to do, buying you time, creating procrastination, until you are forced to make a decision out of necessity.

Here's another example. Let's say you've applied for a job position and have already gone to your first interview. It seemed to go well and you were told that you would be contacted in a week for a second interview. It's been barely a week, and you are starting to lose sleep. When are they going to call? You know darn well that this particular company is pretty formal in their approach and wouldn't look fondly on a preemptive, over-anxious phone call from you. Waiting another day or so sounds like a good option. You're worried and perplexed and starting to lose your confidence. You ask a friend what to do, saying, "I'm so confused, should I wait a couple of days or should I call?" Your friend really has no clue, but suggests waiting might be the better option. Were you really confused? No, you actually knew exactly what to do, but you didn't like it. Waiting a few more days was the right thing to do, but was damn uncomfortable. It had barely been a week, but your insecurity was raging and creating a tug-of-war with your Gut.

If you don't understand, then you're confused. If you do understand and refuse to decide, then you probably don't like your options.

Make Confusion Your Friend

Most of the time confusion is not real. And when you say you're confused, you're probably not. So how do you get out of the confusion habit and into decision-making? Make confusion your friend. When you catch yourself using the confusion excuse, stop and take a better look.

Ask yourself,

⊛ Do I know my options?
⊛ Do I know what I want?

If you know your options and you don't like them, take a better look. Maybe there are options you haven't thought of, yet. Perhaps your Gut has already pointed to the right option and you just need to hear it. If you're truly confused, use your Head and get your facts together. Then let your Gut decide. Confusion will disappear in the face of truth. Confusion is often a smoke screen obscuring a truth you don't want to see. Perhaps seeing it will require you to do something uncomfortable, but necessary. Perhaps you will have to make a sacrifice in order to get your desired result.

People also use the confusion excuse when they don't want to do something they know is right. "Gee, I found this big briefcase full of money by the side of the road. I'm so confused, what I should do with it?" Hmmm. Let's see. Taking it to the police and letting them find the rightful owner or solve a crime sounds like a good idea. Perhaps you'll even get a reward.

This doesn't mean you won't let your mind whirl around picturing yourself with gobs of found cash. This example is not a subtle one, but you get the picture. Doing the right thing is always obvious; we sometimes just don't want to do it.

Confusion exists when your Gut is telling you what to do while your Head is arguing with you. It cannot exist unless you have an emotional attachment to an outcome. When your Heart enters into debate, in service of the Head, confusion flourishes.

If you're confused, unsure if it's you're Head or your Gut suggesting a solution, look to the possible outcome. If it's your Gut talking, the outcome will not be part of the equation. Your Gut will say, "Do this; it's right." Your Head will say something different regarding the outcome. Your Head will say, "Do this, because then this, this, and this will probably happen." If your Head is talking, there is a defined, perceived outcome. If your Heart is speaking to you, there is a feeling behind the choice, most likely with anxiety and concern attached.

Fear is also a component of confusion, and fear is the domain of your Head. When you worry about making the right choice, you automatically need more time to analyze and research your options. It drags on, procrastination sets in, and anxiety rises. Your Gut doesn't work that way. It never makes a "wrong" choice. Confusion is kept alive by an agenda—the agenda of your Head.

A Traffic Accident: An Example of Your Gut Functioning

Here's an example of how your Gut functions when true fear has entered a situation. Let's say you're driving on the highway and an accident quickly unfolds in front of your eyes. A car in front of you swerves to miss another vehicle making an unsafe lane change. The swerving car hits the soft shoulder, skids, and rolls several times, finally coming to a stop on its side. You pull over and jump out of your car, cell phone in hand, moving quickly to the crash scene. You're afraid, but you're moving on instinct. You dial 911 while simultaneously assessing the situation. Once you reach the car you can see that the driver and passenger are conscious, shaken, but not badly injured.

They need help to get out of the vehicle, but things look okay. Instinctively, you reach out your hand as the driver climbs out the window. He's okay. The passenger follows. You help them away from the car and sit with them in the ivy on the side of the road. Help has begun to arrive. Everything's going to be fine.

When you were in the moment, you knew exactly what to do and you did it. You didn't stop to think about how you might be in danger. You didn't keep on driving in hope that someone else would stop. You didn't fail to offer your hand fearing the driver would later sue you for injuring him. You knew there were others who passed by the scene and didn't give a second look. You followed your Gut. Your Head kept you aware of the facts and your Heart gave you the compassion to back up your choice.

Having courage under fire is sometimes easier than having courage when there is no immediate threat.

That's the challenge with many decisions you'll encounter. When there is no life and death consequence in your face, it's so easy to fall into the trap of analysis and confusion.

Your Gut Goes Straight to the Bull's-Eye

Remember, your Head wants to figure it all out and make sure nothing bad happens. Your Gut wants to go straight to the bull's-eye and get to the point. But sometimes your Head doesn't want to do it so it argues its reasons, justifications and logic to convince you it's safe to ignore your Gut.

Occasionally, things work out well despite the intervention of your Head against your Gut. But more frequently, once you've ignored your Gut you end up uttering those famous last words, "I knew I shouldn't have done that." Decisions always break down to your Head and Heart vs. your Gut.

Your Head is about survival, freedom from pain and instant gratification. It pre-judges and is very myopic. It doesn't have the vision your Gut has, and your Head wants proof. So we'll hide behind confusion to buy ourselves time hoping that our Gut answer will change. When we deny truth (the voice of our Gut), we'll suffer regret or consequence.

Emotional attachment to any situation leads to confusion. As I've said, when someone says, "I'm confused; I don't know what to do," they just don't like their options. One way to combat confusion is to accept the worst possible outcome. People think if they do accept the possibility of the worst outcome, then it will happen. It rarely does. Just say, "Okay, what's the worst case scenario?" Face your fear. When you can imagine the worst possible scenario, it will release the emotional attachment and fear of the situation so the best result can take place.

Emotional attachment indicates there's an agenda present. You have an attachment to an outcome. This means you're expecting a payoff. You want things to work out a certain way. When you're in tune with your Gut there isn't any fear, confusion or expectation. When you're attached to your payoff and you're arguing with your Gut, it means you've lost your trust in your inner voice.

The Job Search: An Example of Your Head vs. Your Gut

If you are focused on a potential payoff instead of focusing on what you know is right, you're in your Head. A payoff sounds like this: if I do X, then I will get Y. If you typically use this formula in life, then you, my friend, are in your Head. If your Gut has told you what to do and you start wondering if you'll get your payoff, you're analyzing and justifying your actions.

Let's say you're looking for a new job. You've just started your search and you have set your sights on a particular company. They've offered you a position, but it's really not the right one for your talents and abilities. You say to yourself, "Maybe I should take it anyway. Maybe another position will open up that suits me better and I'll be able to jump on it since I'm already employed by them." You're emotionally attached to working for this firm. Something deep inside tells you, "Don't accept the position," but you want your payoff now. You're justifying doing something you know you shouldn't do.

If you catch yourself justifying an action, it's your Head that's in charge. Your Gut never justifies anything. Get familiar with the language so you will recognize the subtle sound of your Gut no matter how loudly the Head is screaming. It's easier to trust your Gut when you don't have an emotional attachment to an outcome. It's even more important to trust your Gut when it isn't easy to do.

Your Gut makes one-sentence truths; your Head asks questions and makes up multi-sentence excuses and explanations. Your Gut does not have to explain itself. When your Gut decides, you feel calm and neutral. It's an, "I'm okay with either outcome" attitude. No emotional attachment or agenda.

Exercise: Think of a decision you've been pondering and review these questions:

- Did you get a "hit" from your Gut in the beginning? If so, what was it?
- What's your motivation?
- Are you concerned about what other people will think of your choice?
- Are you focusing on your potential payoff?
- Is your choice based on money or some other perceived benefit?
- Is there fear around your choice?

- Do you know your options?
- Do you like your options?
- Will your choice keep your integrity intact?
- Will you be selling off part of your Soul if you make a certain choice?
- Are you choosing out of complacency?
- Are you trying to maintain the status quo as part of your choice?
- Is inertia keeping you from making your choice?
- Are you leaning towards a certain choice because of its predictability?

Truth:

If you're confused and arguing with yourself about what to do, you're probably concerned with your payoff. Expectation, motivation, agenda, ego and attachment come from your Head. Debating about taking the easy way out is also your Head. Your Head will keep you vacillating. Your Gut doesn't vacillate. Your Gut does not go back and forth nor does it use pros and cons. There are no second thoughts when dealing with your Gut.

Trust your Gut as if your life depends on it. It is God whispering to you. Sit where you are and go into your Soul, into your Gut. You will hear God more clearly.

Here's a great quote from Neil Simon about his best advisor, his Gut:

"It's a dangerous thing to turn power over to someone else. You've got to trust yourself. There are so many people who'll say no to what you're doing. Even in the face of that lack of encouragement, if you feel it's good, you have to persevere. There probably aren't too many experts out there who know more about what you're doing than you do."

Be an Observer

When confused, step back from the situation and take a look from the outside in. Detach from any desired outcome and be willing for the truth and answer to emerge. How can you tell if you're not willing? Anxiety will be present as a result of you trying to control the outcome. Whenever you have an attachment you're not willing. Life is easier, really, when you're willing and observing.

There is power in standing back and getting a broader view of your life circumstances. Most often we create drama in our lives by making choices from our Head. Being an observer aids in not creating agendas and emotional attachments to outcomes. Objectivity and neutrality are easier to maintain.

Stand back, listen, breathe and then wait. The next step will come to you. The power in being an observer is that we don't impulsively act on our agendas and emotional attachments, thus the margin of regret and consequence narrows. Clarity ensues. There is personal power and confidence in silence, taking a step back, having faith, being patient and listening.

Examples of Being An Observer:

Not getting caught up in the drama: Don't create something that isn't necessary just to avoid doing what you know to do.

Objectivity: Being objective is less emotional and controlling and always a winning approach.

Neutrality: Being neutral can be difficult because it takes away the power for you to invent situations. Have a clear Someday Vision and be neutral about how to achieve it.

Less is More: Making Gut decisions is very simple and quick. The more difficult you make the circumstances the longer it will take to reach your goals.

Signature Vocabulary/Signature Response: Know and be aware of your Signature Responses and Vocabulary. It will portend what you are drawing into your life and also reveal why you might be stuck.

Active Listening/Absorbing: Being an active listener is a subtle art that enhances your sense of relationship to another and also a deeper understanding and communication. It also increases confidence.

Impartial Listening: To listen impartially is to have no critical commentary while listening or judging what the other person is saying.

<u>Self-observing vs. Self-serving</u>: Stepping back, and observing yourself in any situation will place you in an objective position whereas if you don't then you are immersed in the situation and will find angles to be self-serving.

<u>Silent Observer vs. Dramatic</u>: Truly powerful and confident people are quiet and use fewer words. They don't get caught up in emotional situations or try to control others.

<u>Empowering vs. Disempowering</u>: Each day we have many moments to act in an empowering way or a disempowering way. Observe if you get caught up in drama and what your pattern is so you can catch yourself the next time.

<u>Be in the world though not of it</u>: This is another version of being an observer.

<u>Do the opposite</u>: We have such a habitual nature that real change can only take place if we do the opposite. For example, instead of procrastinating, act

<u>Intention is more powerful than words or actions.</u> It's good to state your clear intentions but don't control the steps you think it will take to make them happen.

Willingness

Willingness leads to Grace
Grace leads to Knowingness
Knowingness leads to Perfect Providence

An attitude of willingness is key to profound change and fulfillment in your life. Willingness releases grace and mercy into your life. Having faith and allowing a "higher force" to guide you can remind you that you don't have to do it all by yourself. Be willing. Be open.

Willingness is embodied in the following statement: "When the student is ready, the teacher will appear." We do receive immense help from the Heavens that will propel us to the heights of satisfaction in our lives.

So what exactly is willingness? It is the opposite of control. Inherent in willingness is trust. Trusting that the Heaven's and God will step in and show you the plan for your life. This isn't to say you should do nothing on your own behalf. It's about openness and faith. Just having willingness is the point. It is surrendering and accepting at the same time, expressing trust and courage at once.

Often when people miss the mark they end up saying, "I guess it's just God's Will." Don't blame God for your failures. Most likely, it was a lack of willingness, or your Free Will that got in the way, not God.

"I am willing to live my purpose; the reason I am here."

This is one of the most liberating and fruitful statements one can make. Let your Soul express.

You must be dedicated to living a meaningful life with no attachment to fame or fortune. Then all that you have to do is your part, God will take care of the rest. Allow yourself to recognize your talents, gifts, interests, desires and dreams. Embrace your visions of the future.

When you practice your skills, express your talents and live a balanced life you create a space for synchronicity to occur. You will find you are simply at the right place at the right time and your life will unfold beautifully.

"To the question of your life, you are the only answer. To the problems of your life, you are the only solution." ~Jo Coudert, American TV executive

The Power Willingness

Having willingness and being an observer works well. If you can be an observer then being willing is easier. What are we to be willing for? We are to be willing that what we feel compelled to do or not to do will feel better and be the better choice in the long run. Even when it seems that we are leaving money or opportunity on the table. Even if others can make the money or take advantage of the opportunity and we have to sit back, trust and wait for our time. When we're 100% willing to listen to our Gut and do what it says - grace and mercy finally, have something to do. Be willing to trust your knowingness. Acknowledge your fear and in spite of it make the choice to go with your Gut.

⊙ Be willing to trust, know and believe your Gut it is the voice of your Soul.

- Commit to be willing to remember your Soul's mission; know why you are here.
- An attitude of willingness is key to profound change and fulfillment in your life.
- Willingness releases Grace and Mercy into your life so you don't have to do it all.

Control

How is it that people find themselves and elements of their lives out of control? How can a relationship get so bad? Their finances get so bad? How can they wake up one day and realize they are miserable in their lives? Is the world a big ugly place out to get them? What is the genesis of their problems? The answer? It is how they made their decisions. From what they thought they would be doing and where they ended up. Stop. Write your vision of your life. How do you see your life in the big scheme of things? How would you like to live? Realistically. Sure, a lot of us would like to win the lottery, be raised in wealthy, privileged and functioning homes. Well, that's usually not the case and even if it were there would be another set of problems stemming from that, too. Take charge of your life; stand up for your vision—your dream life. It's yours to dream, achieve and begin. How do you make decisions? What are you afraid of having, losing, risking, being, doing? You have to live with it. Life is not one big circumstance. It's many conscious and unconscious choices. That's where to begin. Choices. Now let's learn to choose what we want in our lives.

Willingness is the Opposite of Control

When you are really willing then the Universe can step in and show you the plan for your life. The point is just being willing. Willingness is surrendering and accepting at the same time and expressing trust and courage at once. The most liberating and fruitful statement one can make: "I am willing to live the reason I am here".

The Breadcrumbs

Anxiety is present where willingness is absent. When we're willing then anything is possible. When we're not willing fully, then we only see what we decide is best and possible and then we attach ourselves to it. We're too myopic in our vision and have no comprehension as to what is truly possible for us. I suggest following the breadcrumbs.

The Breadcrumbs are a series of commands and clues as to what to do to get what you want. For instance, a breadcrumb is a "DO". It's a simple statement to do something with no explanation given. So, if you have a directive and you follow it then another will be given. They are all based on your desire for something in your life and the breadcrumbs are clues as to your desires. The problem arises when we think (dangerous to do) we know where the remaining crumbs are leading us and we take over leading ourselves off the right path.

Stick to following your Gut breadcrumbs and believe in yourself. Expect the impossible to happen. Realize that if you think you know where you're headed you just jumped in front of the last breadcrumb. Go back to your Someday Vision to re-inspire yourself to stay on track. Each day we're responsible for doing our part. If we're told where we're headed in life we would judge it and most likely reject it.

Try not to worry what your life is going to look like, be more concerned with how you want it to feel.

When we're motivated to live a meaningful life with no attachment to fame or fortune, then all we have to do is our part and the rest will be taken care of. The clues to areas of preparation can be recognized in our talents, gifts, interests, desires and dreams (visions of our future). When we practice our skills, express our talents and live a fairly balanced life (not doing what we shouldn't be doing and doing what we should be doing) then it is a matter of synergy and we'll be in the right place at the right time and our life will begin to unfold beautifully.

Chapter 7

The Language of Your Head, Heart and Gut Recapped

The Language of Your Head

Have you ever heard a song and it stuck in your head and played over and over again? After a while hearing it gets annoying and harder to make it stop. This is much like the Head when it is weighing various options of a decision over and over again.

Let's continue and use a song as an analogy to aid in identifying the voices of your Head, your Heart, and your Gut. Your Head is the melody of the song, very wordy, repeats itself and wants you to remember what it is saying. Your Gut on the other hand has no agenda. It is the steady beat to keep the melody on track. In fact, the bass in music is what actually leads the melody and holds the song together.

For a quick refresher, think of your Head as the melody and chorus while your Gut holds the beat. Your Gut keeps the melody on track and is, in essence, the foundation and leader of the melody. Your Head likes to be the star of the show and take all the credit, when in truth, no song is complete without the sureness of timing.

The voice and language of your Head is going to be very familiar to you. It has several characteristics. When you are listening to the chatter in your Head, it will be in the form of questions and sentences.

For instance,

- What will people think if I...?
- What will my mother say?
- Isn't that a little extravagant?
- Who do you think you are?
- What if I'm wrong?
- I tried that it didn't work.
- It's better to be safe than sorry.

It will also take on stalling tactics such as:

- Manipulation
- Attachment
- Analysis
- Excuses
- Explanations
- Justification
- Rationalization

When in your Head, these will come into play.

Questions: You will ask yourself questions that begin with:

- What if?
- But how?
- Why?

You'll keep repeating these questions over and over hoping the answer will miraculously change. This is the quickest way to recognize you're operating from your Head.

Sentences: You will hear yourself speaking in sentences. Sentences that are long-winded and lead you to ask more questions before you feel ready to decide. Remember, if you're in this state the answer has already been given.

Because: When you are talking and hear yourself utter the word 'because' you are most definitely in your Head. Your Gut never gives a 'because'; only your Head and Heart do.

Stalling tactics: Stalling tactics include finding ways to manipulate the facts so you can justify doing what you think you want to do instead of doing what you know to be the right thing to do. For example, a stalling tactic would be, "I'm not going to return their call yet. I want to wait until after the weekend. It's their fault I have to do this in the first place."

When someone is stalling, they're trying to deflect responsibility from themselves. They may blame someone else for their situation or render themselves helpless to remedy it. Don't be fooled when you or someone else does this.

Explanations and excuses: We can make a career out of doing this. The bottom line is you know on a Gut level what to do, and you're still trying to buy time so you don't have to do it.

Emotional attachment: Your Head becomes emotionally attached to what it thinks it wants. It fixates on an outcome and becomes myopic. As the attachment deepens, emotions become intensified. Having attachment to an outcome sets you up for disappointment and missed opportunities because you're too myopic.

Agenda: In most every situation, your Head has an agenda. Rarely does it operate as an open mind, no pun intended. The only time it's okay to act on an agenda is when your Gut sanctions it. An agenda is deciding in advance what the outcome will be, and then becoming fixated on it. The error in doing that is you forfeit the best outcome. Life changes second by second. Rarely does a situation follow a straight path. It twists, turns and detours before it reaches completion. Trust the mystery of it all.

Fear-based: Your Head is Fear Central. It gains confidence following a logical route, and becomes insecure having faith in the unknown. It expects and anticipates the worst outcome. Your Head likes to have an agenda and is completely fear-based.

Justifying and rationalizing: Now, if you've reached this point, you're probably in a fair amount of conflict. One thing is guaranteed—you'll regret going this far and you'll suffer consequences for taking this route. **Manipulating** events falls in this category, as well. Trying to control others and circumstances always backfires.

I know that last one sounded pretty eerie, but it's true. This isn't to scare you, but to explain why you cringe at the thought of bad decisions you made in the past. The choices that made you ask yourself, "How did I let it go that far?" Or, "Why didn't I just do what I knew I should've done? I created a mess out of that one. I knew I shouldn't have done that," and so on.

Don't get me wrong; your Head has its strengths but knowing the best decision is not one of them. Being the leader is not one of them, either. How comforting is it to have a fearful leader, anyway?

Okay, on to your Heart.

☺

The Language of Your Heart

It has already been established that your Heart is not a good leader or decision maker.

Your Heart is good for backing your Gut. The voice of your Heart can sound like a range of emotions such as sadness, fear, anger, joy, depression, guilt and excitement.

When your Heart is talking, you'll hear yourself saying something like this:

- But I love him.
- I don't want her to feel bad.
- That was awful, I'd better help.
- I feel bad about firing him.
- I can't stop seeing her; she'll fall apart.
- I know he's bad for me, but we have great chemistry.

Any sentence that evokes pity, sympathy or worry for how someone is feeling or how they will cope is your Heart's domain. Now, being concerned about others is nice, but not when it's placed over and above doing the right thing.

Not every decision will be a feel-good choice for us. Taking the easy way out short changes unknown possibilities and potential in the long run. Try to stand brave in the face of unpleasant or painful choices. It builds character and is always worth it. Trust me; the process works.

The Language of Your Gut

Now, let's move on to the best part.

Once you recognize the feel, language and voice of your Gut, you'll not be able to ignore it. Your Gut grows stronger the more you acknowledge it.

Using your Gut is a bit like working your muscles when you exercise. The more you use them, the stronger they get and the more you can count on your new strength.

After a few times of listening to and acting on your Gut, you'll easily recognize the language and not be able to deny it. At times, you might even rue the day you read this book, and look back on the saying "ignorance is bliss" with new regard.

I'm just kidding. Well, kind of. Following your Gut is akin to having your conscience in high gear. Remember the Jim Carey movie Liar, Liar? In the movie, Carey's character is stricken with a hyper-aware conscience after his son made a potent wish that his dad wouldn't tell another lie.

Suddenly, everything Carey's character says is the brutal honest truth. At first, he's horrified at his lack of control. His Head is telling him the words to say and his mouth takes over and he can't lie. He has to speak the truth. In the end it all works out. The truth-telling has turned his life into one with meaning.

That movie is a humorous illustration of hearing one's Gut all the time. Now, of course you won't experience it to that degree. But, it gives you an idea of how, once you hear your Gut, you'll be able to decipher it from the voice and language of your Head and your Heart pretty quickly.

Learning this makes life less stressful. You'll feel more confident moving through the unexpected events that go against what you thought would have happened.

Also, going with your Gut has an interesting way of setting you up to be in the right place at the right time for something to happen that you'll be happy about. In fact, many who have learned to go with their Gut say that if they *hadn't* follow their Gut, certain events could not have taken place at all. They would have missed opportunities.

It's too hard to judge which occurrences are the key ones to take us where we want to be in life. If you stay true to your Gut, you'll be happy with where you are. It won't let you down. You won't have to live an austere life or be a goody two-shoes, either. It's just a smart and simple shortcut for making all the right choices.

Just as I did for your Head and your Heart, below I have listed basic principles for following your Gut. Remember, you don't have to have any special skill or lifestyle to be able to hear and follow your Gut. With practice, it will soon become second nature.

Here are a few more tips for knowing you're hearing your Gut:

Your Gut speaks in statements that are made of five words or less. This is crucial to know. The wordier the answer, the more apt it's your Head or your Heart influencing you. If you remember anything in this book, remember - **five words or less.**

It will sound like a command. Some examples may be:

- ☺ Don't marry him.
- ☺ Cancel those plans.
- ☺ Look for a new job.

Your Gut won't give you a reason why to do or not to do something. If the words "because," "why," or "how" are present in your vocabulary, it's not your Gut speaking, but rather your Head and/or your Heart.

Your Gut won't go into detail. It's incessant and won't stop even if you try to ignore it. It's very patient and can hold out longer than even the most stubborn person.

Here are examples of what your Gut might say to you. They can be heard at any moment during the day on any topic, experience or circumstance. Every moment and situation has a Gut message.

For example, see if you've heard or spoken any of these:

- I know this is right.
- I'd better do this.
- He's not the one.
- Don't do it.
- Call her now.
- Turn here.
- Don't do that.
- This feels right.
- I want this.
- I have to leave.

The statements are always five words or less, concise and simple. You know you're in your Head when the sixth word is 'because' and the language becomes more complicated and repetitive. Five words or less is a truth, and six words or more means you're trying to make something true that isn't.

When your Gut is speaking, you should feel calm and centered and that things are okay, not anxious. The message will always be simple, clear and insistent.

Truth:

If you're not listening to your Gut, then you're listening to either your Head or your Heart. Your Heart is a follower, not a leader. Your Head is the justifier and will have an agenda and an emotional attachment to the outcome. One way to know if you're listening to your Head is if you're feeling confused.

Why don't we listen to our Gut all the time? Because it takes courage and it's usually a blind road. You won't be given any details just the vision—the big picture. You'll have to trust each step as it's presented to you. And at first, that can be scary.

Your Gut is courage-based: Your Gut has no fear. It's completely neutral. It takes on forgiveness of the past and has confidence in the future. With your Gut leading, there is no unsure step, even around a blind corner.

Your Gut is neutral: Your Gut has no agenda or emotional attachment to any outcome. It is simply a messenger.

Your Gut is faith: If your Gut is telling you to make a change in your life, its main concern is not going to be your level of comfort. It knows what lies ahead. Your Gut is faith and is most potent in the present. Don't worry about the future—it's being handled each moment of every day.

Your Gut is an observer: It is calm. It is patient. It is faith. It trusts blindly. These are great qualities to possess. Your Gut takes on a bigger view of your life and circumstances. It knows you will be all right even if you feel uncomfortable. It knows better than your Head what you want and what is best for you. It takes discipline to trust your Gut. It takes discipline and patience to live a life of potential.

When You Make Life Changes, Trust Your Gut

Again, if your Gut is telling you to make a change in your life, its main concern is not going to be your level of comfort. It knows what lies ahead. Your Gut has faith in you and believes in your future.

The problem is we don't give our Gut credit when we most need its guidance to move us forward.

Always remember, it matters not what you decide, but how you made the decision.

"I always go with my Gut because my Gut is the only thing I really know. There are a lot of things I can't do because I don't have the Gut for it. I never second-guess the Gut. The only time I second-guess is when I'm not operating from the Gut." —Oprah

A Few Reminders

See, I told you it's not hard to hear your Gut. The key is to get familiar with the language of each: your Head, Heart and Gut, and then listen, trust, and act on it. In fact, you don't have to trust it, just act. Trust will develop quickly on its own.

I wrote this next section as a quick reference tool. It has several reminders to help keep you on track in trusting your Gut. If I'm repeating myself, consider it repetition for emphasis.

Here I'll also cover a big issue—time. When making a decision, time is a big factor. There are two sides to time: action and procrastination.

For example:

- You run into trouble when you don't give your Gut credit when you most need its guidance to move you forward.
- Just because you know the right answer doesn't mean we have to act on it immediately (though eventually, circumstances lead you to).
- Simply acknowledging the right choice can oftentimes be enough. Denial and resistance take a lot of effort.

If you procrastinate on doing what you know needs to be done, eventually your hand will be forced and it most likely won't be pleasant.

Usually you have too much time to make big decisions. This can be a double-edged sword. Even though you have time to breathe, the more time you have, the more dialoguing and arguing your Head and Heart will do with you.

Critical, high intensity decisions are the easiest to make. The answer screams louder and you are more sensitive to it. In fact, you trust those more because our Head and Heart don't have time to interfere or muddy the waters.

Check in with your Gut to determine the best time to act on its guidance.

Your Head is to carry out your Gut's choice and your Heart is to put the emotion or passion into it. If you follow your Gut, your Head is free to add important data and details, and your Heart is free to supply the emotion, enthusiasm and sentiment.

Your Gut tells you where to go. It's your GPS taking you where you really want to go, not where you think you want to go. Your Head drives the car, and your Heart listens to the radio, enjoys the scenery, and cherishes the experience.

When your Head is talking, it speaks in questions and sentences that start with, "how," "what if," "why," and "but." Chaos and confusion happen when your Gut is telling you what to do and your Head is arguing with you.

☉ If you're confused, that's good news, really! One can't be confused without knowing the answer. When people say they're confused, it means they know what to do—they just don't want to do it.

"It's a dangerous thing to turn power over to someone else," Neil Simon said. "You've got to trust yourself. There are so many people who'll say no to what you're doing. Even in the face of that lack of encouragement, if you feel good, you have to persevere. There probably aren't too many experts out there who know more about what you're doing than you do."

Your Track Record

Now that you've learned how to recognize and act on your Gut, you can keep track of your successes and challenges until you, too, master following your Gut.

Grab a notebook or journal and keep a running list of decisions you're facing from the small, less critical to the life-changing. Soon you'll begin to see your default pattern. We all have a default mechanism and make the majority of decisions from our Head or our Heart. Are you more analytical or emotional? By knowing what that pattern is makes it easier to acknowledge and trust your Gut.

When you begin going with your Gut, you will quickly become so familiar with it you can't forget it. Once you get used to hearing the questions of your Head and the statements of your Gut, you won't need to write them down to distinguish them. They're truly different in their language and the feeling they elicit in you.

My Wish For You

Ever since New Year's Eve 1996, I have been living from my Gut. I've ignored my Gut, and I've followed my Gut. And I've learned that my life always falls into place when I go with my Gut. I haven't always liked the answers I've heard in the moment, but I have learned that I really don't like the outcome of a Head or Heart choice that went against my Gut.

In writing this book, I've become convicted in the truth and validity of my Gut and respect others for their Gut Knowingness, too.

Our Head and Heart don't know the *big picture* of who we are and what we're truly capable of, *but,* our Gut does. If we follow it step-by-step throughout our day, we have the best chance of living our life to its fullest potential.

My wish for you ... Go With Your Gut and live out your destiny.

Your Gut Moments

I receive emails from people who have heard my presentation on *Go With Your Gut*. They write to me relaying their Gut Moments. If you have any moments when you have taken a chance on your Gut, I would love to hear about it.

Please send them to me via email at:
Mary@GoWithYourGut.net

Visit http://www.GoWithYourGut.net for more information on my *Go With Your Gut* presentation, and to order more copies of the book.

Become a Fan on Facebook:
http://www.facebook.com/gowithyourgut

Tools for Accessing

Your Gut

It was a good day when I learned a trick to change my frame of mind. I also realized the importance of being in the right frame of mind when it came to making clear and correct choices. I call it Spiritual Sustenance. We give out so much energy and thoughts throughout the day and our schedules are so hectic and demanding, we need to find a way to rejuvenate ourselves from the inside out to handle the stress and make the best decisions. If we don't it begins to take a toll on our confidence. We've all been through rough times, but when you have nowhere to go to lift yourself up, the challenges are a lot harder. When negative thoughts or outer pressures are ruling your thoughts it's difficult to hear the voice of your Gut. The answers are there you just need to refuel your sense of self to hear them.

The reality is you're going to feel good about your life and bad about your life about eight times a day. That might seem an extreme statement but think about it. If you're in business you might gain a new client, settle a conflict with another client or lose a client all in the same day. Now, don't forget the person who waved a single finger at you on the road as you drove to work or the crabby grocery clerk you encountered. On top of that the stress of bills and the many responsibilities and demands we face each day. It is imperative to rejuvenate yourself in order to hear your Gut clearly.

To stop dwelling on a problem there are many options you can choose from. Depending on the amount of time you have and inspiration you need, you could:

- Read a meaningful quote
- Read an inspiring book
- Get some aerobic exercise.

Other ideas to be in a place to hear your Gut and feed your Soul include Spiritual Sustenance from:

- Listening to a song collection
- Reading a verse from the Bible
- Doing some yoga poses, going for a run, or deep breathing.

These activities are a good place to start to get back in your body and get you out of your Head. They're also for when you know you're out of balance and need a boost. It's good preventative care for your Soul, too. Find what works for you and do it with gusto when you know you need a fix. Changing your state will give you a more realistic perspective of your life. It's a drink from a glass that is half-full. It's an affirmation that you are forcing yourself out of a dark, lonely, sad, hopeless, or frightened mood. You'll know you've found your vehicle when it works quickly and every time. Try it. You have nothing to lose and everything to gain.

Here are a few other ideas to know that are helpful:

Preparation + Opportunity = Luck
We've seen that slogan before, now let's define it. Preparation is practicing our talents, taking care of our health and handling the Big Four—spiritual, physical, mental, and emotional aspects of our lives—in the most balanced way possible.

The Universe is in charge of opportunity. If we're not prepared, then all of the opportunities in the world will mean nothing. For example, having a talent for singing and not practicing or writing and then not being prepared when an opportunity comes up to audition for a band—you then missed an opportunity.

Luck
When you've had the courage to admit who you are and when you are committed to your mission, act on your purpose and you are willing to be of service to others.

Self-Doubt
Self-doubt is the Genesis of Fear. One only has to doubt the truth of who they are to allow fear in. Self-knowingness, confidence and assuredness leave no

room for fear to come in. Free Will is fear-based and speaks in doubt of most everything. Ask yourself, what do you doubt about yourself? Do you doubt that you can't find happiness in your Soul pursuits? The mere fact that you doubt is the reason for your soul aching. We can walk into the face of fear and beyond but it's more prudent to squash doubt. Doubt will make us walk with wobbly knees. Sometimes we're afraid and do it anyway. Doubt in yourself will make you so unsure you will barely be able to breathe. Fear is not bad; it gives one an edge and promotes courage. Self-doubt is useless. There is no positive outcome to self-doubt. It is the passive tormenter.

Isolation and Letting Your Soul Breathe

Isolation is how we compartmentalize the Universe. We call on the Universe when we're in a crisis and at the first sign of guidance we say, "I'm good, I'll take it from here."

And we go back to our normal way of navigating through the maze of our life. The guidance and direction you receive from your Gut and the Universe is trying to help you remember your Soul's path. Guidance is inside you, around you and beyond you. Have a sense of duty to your Soul. Let it live, breathe, give it a chance to live and breathe. How does that look? It looks like art. It sounds like an honest conversation. It feels like an earnest effort at birthing (anything). It sweats like ambition in the sweltering sun. It is rich and tangible. It is inner peace.

Bonus Chapter

The Soul of Your Gut

In this bonus chapter, I want to present a deeper level of what we've been covering thus far. As I've said, I believe our Gut instinct and knowingness is our Soul voice trying to guide us to a life we inherently desire to live.

Through my research, studies and personal experiences, I believe our Soul is infinite and we tap into only a fraction of it. There is an abundance of who we truly are, and it feeds us knowledge and desire, and is the wisdom and guidance for us to live most authentically. If we listen to our Gut, we're actually listening to our Soul. It is pure, unique guidance just for you.

Desire is the Clue to Your Destiny

So what about desire? Desire to do certain work when you have a vision for your life. Where does that come from? Certainly not your Head. Everyone has wants that have no relationship to anything having to do with their Soul's path. True desire is not superficial.

It's a deep and powerful need coming directly from the core of your being.

Your Soul's Will plants the seed of your desires. Following your Soul's Will ensures that you will have or create what you desire. Desire is not a mental process; it's a Soulful process. Your life path is not a mental process, either. If you choose a mental process to map out your life you will stumble and fail unnecessarily.

One way to bring to life your desires is to create what I call a Someday Vision. We all have dreams and desires and they actually come through us; we don't think them up. We may believe we do, but we don't. They're an innate part of us and our Gut/Soul is feeding us clues all the time about what they are. Oftentimes, we may daydream about the possibility of living life in a certain way, and other times we think our current life can't support the pursuit of those dreams.

It is real. Take a look at Oprah, Shakira and I'm sure I can find hundreds of stories of inspiration where people had a Someday Vision about their life and their Gut/Soul guided them to achieving it. It's a part of who they are. It's a vision they saw themselves living and they believed in it. They knew it was their destiny.

Dare to Dream

I encourage you to dare to dream and really admit what your Someday Vision is. Julia Child wrote her first book at 49 and started her television show at 51. There is time for you to live your destiny.

Here are a few ways to jumpstart your vision:

- Remember back to when you were 18 years old or younger. What did you dream you wanted to do with your life?
- What hobbies or interests did you have?
- Go through magazines and cut out phrases, pictures and words that resonate with your authentic self and create a collage of it. If you can clearly visualize it and admit it, then it's more likely to happen.

Truth:
The more you can see and feel your vision, the faster it will magnetize to you. You won't have to think up how to create it.

Your Soul vs. Your Personality

Now that I have given a brief definition of Soul, I want to clarify the difference between your Soul and your personality.

There is a distinct difference between living your Soul's path versus acting on your personality. Your Soul has a pure and perfect blueprint of you and who you are fully capable of being. It houses your potential and every single step you take, person you meet, circumstance you experience and divine timing. Your Soul uses desire to give you clues as to the passion, skills and talents you have. When someone says they don't know their passion, it means they're out of touch with their Soul.

Your personality is your Ego making decisions about your life. Your personality is the part of you that is shaped by your Head/Ego and your Heart, and has no clue as to your path. Its job is to express what your Soul wants to express. You are not your personality, you're personality is your Soul in action. Have you ever been around someone you felt good around and wanted to spend more time with, something you couldn't explain?

I heard a story about Graeme Green, the journalist. He wanted to meet Padre Pio but he had to wait a year for a fifteen-minute appointment. He arrived in Europe, sat through a Mass, and as he was approaching his time with Padre Pio, he turned, walked out and flew home.

When asked why he walked out when he waited over a year and was so close to meeting Padre Pio and he replied, "I wasn't prepared for how he would change my life."

That, my friend, is an example of a potent Soul, not a personality.

Your Soul is potent and powerful. It is tangible in those who breathe life into it and regard it more than they do their Ego/personality. Your personality is the vehicle to let your Soul shine. Very exciting.

The Difference Between Destiny and Fate

Fate is the verb of our Ego, and Destiny is the verb of our Soul.

Fate is where we were born, who our parents, siblings and relatives are and how we were influenced and shaped by them. It also is where we went to school and who our friends are. It consists of our values, morals, education, and social environment.

Destiny is what our Soul has in store for us.

Unfulfilled people are living out their fate and feel no power in their destiny.

Act on Your Soul's Will, Not on Your Free Will

Be willing to live the reason for which you were born, and your Soul will lead you throughout your day.

There are two ways to live, from either your Free Will or your Soul's Will.

We've all heard about Free Will, and even our parents mentioned we have the Free Will to do whatever we want as an adult as long as we don't do it under their roof.

All kidding aside…

Yes, we have Free Will to do whatever we want, but take into consideration that means we're acting from our Ego which is synonymous with our Head, and that means we're acting from fear and having to think everything up. Whew, that's a lot of pressure.

On the other hand, our Soul's Will is courageous, innate and synonymous with Spirit. Your Soul's nature is not dependent on your circumstances or the conditions of your life. It's the essence of you and it wants to be expressed. Free Will, without the help of your Soul's Will, isn't enough. Free Will is a nice idea, but by definition can convince us to do whatever we want, whether it's right, wrong, good, bad or ugly. Your Soul's Will guides you to the right next step. The best part about Free Will is that we have the Free Will to relinquish Free Will and go back to our Soul's Will.

History and religion have granted us the right to Free Will, and we hold onto it tightly. Free Will is the sacred and inalienable right of every human, so we've been told. We feel Free Will that gives us control and power over our lives and what happens to us. Unfortunately, what most of us are doing with our Free Will is allowing our Heart and our Head to make decisions that are only critical to our emotional and physical safety. But this is a myopic and fearful view.

There's nothing inherently wrong with the concept of Free Will. Truly, you can do whatever you want to do. But your Gut isn't interested in your Free Will. Your Gut wants you to follow your Soul's Will. The purest direction and guidance we have.

> "How wonderful it is to do your will! For that is freedom. There is nothing else that ever should be called by freedom's name. Unless you do your will, you are not free." — Course in Miracles

The goal is to learn to follow your Soul's Will. To do so, you must listen to the voice of your Gut as it speaks to you. No one is taking your Free Will away from you, but your Soul's Will, as expressed by your Gut, is the only way to success.

A Simple Formula
> Head and Heart = Free Will
> Gut = Soul's Will

It's that simple. Yes, you have the right to choose. So choose your Gut!

Many people do what they want to do with their lives, yet fail or come up short in their quest for meaning and fulfillment. This notion perpetuates the belief that it's difficult to know one's path or that finding purpose in life is elusive. It's really not difficult. You do know how you truly want to live. It's how you go about it that's tripping you up. Your Gut will tell you every day and every step of how, if you'll listen.

The mind can never create the life that will satisfy your soul's yearning. It's the lack of courage, confidence and trust in the voice of your Gut that is the starting point of every struggle. You've been trained to have a plan; a map of how you're going to achieve a goal. If you are acting on your Soul's path, you can't create a mental process to achieve it. You must follow the steps laid out by your Soul. Your Soul will only tell you enough to get you to move, yet thankfully, not enough for you to screw up the movement.

Impatience about not knowing all the details or not having a complete picture creates doubt. Instead of waiting for the voice of your Soul, worry sets in. You're afraid of not knowing and this is where you'll falter and take steps that will slow your progress. When you don't know, great! Then you can't screw it up.

It's a discipline to trust that you'll know what to do in the moment. The guidance given through your Gut, in an instance, will give you a yes or no to each opportunity.

Once you can master the process of quickly identifying your Gut response, while keeping your Head and your Heart on the sideline, then Providence, or Divine Guidance and Protection, can step in.

Willingness leads to Grace
Grace leads to Knowingness
Knowingness leads to Perfect Providence

You have the option to live from your Free Will or your Soul's Will. Choosing to live from your Free Will allows you to make your choices the way you think best. God will not interfere with your choices. You can experience whatever you choose to experience in this lifetime. The most fortuitous act of Free Will is having the courage and confidence to relinquish it in order to heed your Soul's Will.

So be who you are, not who you think you should be. If you desire something, go towards it. Desire is a clue as to your path.

Quick Reference

What do you mean by our Gut?

Gut/Soul/God: Depending on the example I am making I interchange these three to mean the same. The Gut is the region of our body our Soul makes itself felt, viscerally. The language it speaks is connected to God, thus guidance. The voice we hear and feel in our Gut is God's and the part of ourselves that takes action is our Soul.

What does our Gut sound like?

Our Gut speaks in statements and commands of five words or less. "Don't do this." "This is right, go ahead." "I want this." It doesn't give you a reason why to do or not to do something. If the words "because", "why", or "how" are present in your vocabulary, it is not your Gut speaking, but your Head or your Heart. It does not go into detail. It is incessant and will not go away even if one ignores it.

How do I know if I'm hearing my Gut?

When your Gut is speaking you will feel calm and centered, not anxious. Things are "Okay". The message is simple, clear and insistent.

Why should I listen to my Gut?
It is the voice of your core. It is akin to listening to God via meditation. It has no agenda but to guide you to living your Soul's Will.

If I am not listening to my Gut then what am I listening to? You're listening to either your Heart or your Head. Your Heart is a follower not a leader. Your Head is the justifier and will have an agenda and be emotionally attached to an outcome. One way to know if you're listening to your Head is if you think you're confused.

Why don't we listen to our Gut all the time?
It takes courage and it's usually a blind road. You won't be given the details just the vision, the big picture. You'll have to trust each step as it's presented to you.

What does my Head sound like?
It speaks in sentences and asks questions. It is fear-based. It analyzes, gives explanations and makes excuses.

What does my Heart sound like?
Your Heart will bring up feelings and insistently push them into your awareness when you're faced with a decision. You'll feel anger, love, compassion, or sympathy welling up and trying to get in the way of your decision. Your Head will usually follow with rationalizations.

What does Willingness have to do with making choices?
Underlying trust is Willingness. One must be willing to trust and act on their Soul's voice if they want to have a satiated soul.

Do I have to be religious to believe in this?
No. This material is not tied to any religion. Although, I am a practicing Catholic and I enjoy topics on spirituality and I practice yoga as well. I speak of the Heaven's/God/The Universe and The Unseen based on my experience and understanding of the material. I am a big believer in our Soul being an active part of our life moment by moment and our Gut is giving us guidance as to our Soul's ultimate expression of service. This is spiritual and practical. It is very exciting to see your Soul's path unfolding.

What do you Mean by Daily Spiritual Sustenance?
Have a plan of action for when you lose faith in the process of your Soul's path. It can include music, exercise, reading or talking with someone. It's an activity that lifts you out of the doldrums within minutes. Only you can control the quality of your day.

The Unseen: This is another way I refer to the Universe or God. It is referred to as the Unseen because it is just that, an invisible force or energy we've become accustomed to giving credit for the myriad coincidences or synchronistic events throughout our day.

The Heavens: Yet another term for where guidance comes from. This term is used when it is obvious the hand of God was pushing you, or the Word of God had a message for you. This may be from a book, a song or during a conversation. Each time it happens it will be just what you needed.

Providence: Providence refers to a state where divine intervention and protection become available. You open yourself up to Providence when you go with your Gut.

Willingness, Initiation, Activation: The miraculous is ordinary. When you are willing you go through a subtle initiation to the new way you will make decisions and choices in your life. That will activate a deeper quality of experience and expression of your Soul. Progressive revelation.

Humanity versus Heavenly: Surrender and go deeper. Practice excavating your fears and expanding your container, which can house more of your Soul. The more Soul energy you contain the less effort you need to expend to make things happen in your life. Your Soul is a magnet for opportunities your mind is a barrier to them. Get underneath the story and pain to reach your Soul.

Acknowledgments

My darling daughters, Sterling and Portia, you are my true inspiration.

Kell, I don't know what I'd do without you. This book definitely would not have been possible without your help and constant nudging. You are a dear friend and colleague. Thank you for being a part of my life.

My sincerest gratitude goes out to Terri Langhans and Mark LeBlanc. Your continued support of the Go With Your Gut process over the years is priceless to me.

Thank you to Frank Dickinson, Marilyn Stafford, and Rick Crespo for your time and valuable feedback on this book. I appreciate all of you.

About Mary Goulet

Mary is the creator of the Go With Your Gut process. Since 1997 she has trusted her Gut to navigate her through life's obstacles and opportunities. Through her books, coaching and speaking Mary is able to guide others on how to consciously make decisions with their gut. Her desire is to give everyone the confidence to make decisions they can trust.

Mary is an award winning author, a recognized brand spokesperson on morning shows nationwide and a voice over actor. She began her career on Wall Street as an institutional bond salesperson followed by owning her own real estate company. She also sang professionally and is currently a licensed holistic health practitioner.

Mary is the co-host of MomsTown® television and co-founder of MomsTown, Inc. As a media personality, Mary has also hosted two radio shows under the *Entrepreneur* magazine brand and co-hosted *Sign On San Diego,* a local news show.

Other books by Mary Goulet

Go With Your Gut: The Art of Making Simple and Critical Decisions
(Rendler Publishing, 2003)

It's All About You: Live the Life You Crave
(Simon & Schuster, 2007)

The MomsTown® Guide To Getting It All:
A Life Makeover For Stay-at-Home Moms
(Hyperion Books, 2005)